BIRDS AND BEES

by Charlie Josephine

||SAMUEL FRENCH||

FOR AMATEUR PRODUCTION ENQUIRIES

UNITED KINGDOM AND WORLD
EXCLUDING NORTH AMERICA
licensing@concordtheatricals.co.uk

020-7054-7298

Each title is subject to availability from Concord Theatricals, depending upon country of performance.

BIRDS AND BEES was commissioned by Theatre Centre and is a co-production between Theatre Centre and Sheffield Theatres. The cast was as follows:

AARRON . . . . Richard Logun
BILLY . . . . Milo McCarthy
LEILAH . . . . Dumile Sibanda
MAISY . . . . Sandra Belarbi

Creative Team

Director	Rob Watt
Sound Designer	Lee Affen
Movement Director	Yami Löfvenberg
Lighting Designer	Hector Murray
Set & Costume Designer	Bethany Wells
Movement Assistant	Elsabet Yonas

Production Team

Resources	Hannah Austin
Marketing for Theatre Centre	Rachel Bellman
Production Manager	Gareth Edwards
Company Stage Manager	Lizzie Bond
Producers for Theatre Centre	Amy Michaels & Emma Rees
Marketing Consultants	Jane Morgan Associates
PR	Chloe Nelkin Consulting & Jo Allan PR
Schools Tour Booking & Coordination for Theatre Centre	Niamh Parker-Whitehead
Casting Consultant	Becky Paris
Artwork	Guy Sanders

CAST & CREATIVE TEAM

Sandra Belarbi (MAISY)
(she/her) Sandra graduated from ALRA/Rose Bruford in 2022. Her stage credits include *Le Morte d'Arthur* (Matthew Evans), *Phaedra* (Sacha Duchamp), *People, Places & Things* (Jane Jeffery), *Rage* (Anastasia Osei-Kuffour), *A Midsummer Night's Dream* (Liam Begin, Paloma Oakenfold), *Boy* (Simon Pittman), *Beat Poetry* (Gemma Aked-Priestley) and *Dance Nation* (Lucy Curtis). Sandra is a very musical person, she loves to play the piano, guitar and ukulele.

Richard Logun (AARRON)
(he/him) Richard is a Nigerian-born actor based in South-East London. Having discovered a love of acting through playing Marius in a secondary school production of *Les Misérables*, he went on to train at Mountview Academy of Theatre Arts, graduating in 2022. His most recent work includes playing the character 'T' in a schools tour of *The Lies You Tell* produced by the New Wolsey Theatre and Theatre Royal Bury St Edmunds.

Milo McCarthy (BILLY)
(they/them) Milo is a non-binary actor who trained at Italia Conti. They recently made their professional debut in Rogers and Hammerstein's *Cinderella* at the Hope Mill Theatre, covering the role of Jean-Michel. Credits include *Starry, The Vincent Van Gogh Musical* (Workshop), *Pippin* (Italia Conti), and *Carrie* (Italia Conti).

Dumile Sibanda (LEILAH)
(she/her) Dumile's most recent work was *Rock, Paper, Scissors* by Chris Bush, a triptych of plays as part of the Sheffield Theatres celebrating fifty years of the Crucible. She graduated from Bristol Old Vic Theatre School. Her credits include playing Thea in *Hedda* on the main stage at Bristol Old Vic, directed by Jenny Stephens, and Nina in *The Three Seagulls* directed by Sally Cookson, also at Bristol Old Vic. Her professional work includes playing Gretel in Insane Root Theatre's production of *Hansel and Gretel*.

Charlie Josephine (Writer)
(they/them) Charlie Josephine is an actor and a writer. Their award-winning work includes *I, Joan*, *Bitch Boxer* and *Massive*. Charlie's passionate about honest, sweaty storytelling that centres working-class women and queer people. They're an associate artist at the NSDF and is this year's Resident Writer at Headlong Theatre. Charlie is currently under commission at the RSC, Salon Pictures and NT Connections.

Rob Watt (Director)

(he/him) Rob Watt is a critically acclaimed queer director, dramaturg and facilitator. He collaborates with writers, young people, communities, poets and designers to make sense of the fractured world we inhabit.

He is currently the Artistic Director for Theatre Centre, regularly teaches at the Royal Central School of Speech and Drama and works with the Institute of the Arts Barcelona. He previously was an Associate for Headlong Theatre, headed up the young people's team at the National Theatre, was a Lead Artist at Lyric Hammersmith, an Artist Mentor at the Barbican and Associate Director at Immediate Theatre.

Selected credits: *Human Nurture* by Ryan Calais Cameron (Theatre Centre & Sheffield Theatres, Theatre Peckham); *C+NTO* by Joelle Taylor (Apples and Snakes); *Acts of Resistance* by Stef Smith (Headlong Theatre & Bristol Old Vic); *Rallying Cry* by Apples and Snakes (Battersea Arts Centre, BBC Contains Strong Words Festival Hull, Brighton Fringe); *The Exorcism* by Ross Sutherland (Battersea Arts Centre); *SEXY* by Vanessa Kisuule (Roundhouse / Bristol Old Vic / UK Tour); *Be Prepared* by Ian Bonar (Underbelly / VAULT Festival); *Party Trap* by Ross Sutherland (Shoreditch Town Hall); *Goosebumps* by Rob Watt (The Vaults); *Standby For Tape Back-Up* by Ross Sutherland (Summerhall / Soho Theatre / Shoreditch Town Hall / UK tour)

Bethany Wells (Set & Costume Designer)

(she/her) Trained in architecture, Bethany is an award-winning performance designer working across dance, theatre and installation, with a particular interest in site-specific and devised performances. She sees all of her work as a form of spatial, social and sensory activism. She is interested in exploring what can be achieved politically and socially by the collective live experience of performance. Her practice is trauma-informed, in terms of both process and audience experience.

Current projects include: *Birds and Bees*, Sheffield Theatres; *All That Lives*, The Grief Series; *The People's Palace of Possibility*, The Bare Project

Recent work includes: *You Heard Me*, Luca Rutherford; *Choreography of Care Symposium*, Claire Cunningham; *Written in the Body*, Charlotte Spencer Projects, Brighton Festival; *This Endless Sea*, Chlöe Smith; *Extreme Unction Vol. 2*, Nwando Ebizie; *War of the Worlds*, Rhum + Clay; *Thank You Very Much*, Claire Cunningham, MIF/National Theatre of Scotland

Hector Murray (Lighting Design)

(he/him) Hector is a lighting designer for plays, dance and musicals working in the UK and internationally.

In 2020 he was nominated for an Offie Award: Best Lighting Designer for his work on *Whistle Down the Wind*. In 2017 he received the ETC Award for excellence in lighting design from the Association of Lighting Designers.

Design credits include: *A Night with Boy Blue* (Barbican Theatre); *Dirty Hearts* (Old Red Lion); *Treasure Island* (Greenwich Theatre); *Kattam Katti* (Sadlers Wells); *1st Luv* (The Big House); *Beige* (The Vaults); *Whistle Down the Wind* (Union Theatre) and *Acts of Resistance* (Headlong Futures)

Lee Affen (Sound Designer)

(he/him) Lee is a composer, music producer, sound designer and theatremaker from Manchester now based in Sheffield. Lee composes for theatre, dance and film, and sonic storytelling and collaboration are at the heart of his practice.

Lee's credits include Cardboard Citizens' *Who Are Yer?*, Imagine If's *Jadek*, Fallen Angels and Birmingham Royal Ballet's *The War Within*, the Theatre Centre and Sheffield Theatre's *Human Nurture*, Roots Mbili's *Fargone*, BBC Radio 3's *New Voices*, the Bare Project's *Outskirts*, Utopia Theatres' *Anna Hibiscus' Song*, the British Library's *Where Two Rivers Meet*, Theatr Clwyd and Paperfinch's *The Fairytale Detectives* and original live scores for *Metropolis*, *Nosferatu* and *The Passion of Joan of Arc*.

Lee is a company member of the Bare Project and an Associate Artist with Imagine If Theatre and Box of Tricks Theatre. 2023 sees Lee working on productions with the Theatre Centre, Box of Tricks, Utopia Theatre and the Bare Project.

Yami Löfvenberg (Movement Director)

(she/her) Yami "Rowdy" Löfvenberg is a multidisciplinary artist, a movement and theatre director, working at the intersection of dance, theatre and cross-arts. Between making her own work, Yami mentors, educates and delivers workshops. She is a lecturer in Hip-Hop and Vernacular Dances at Trinity Laban Dance Conservatoire. A British Council and Arts Council England recipient, Howard Davies Emerging Directors Grant Recipient, One Dance UK DAD Trailblazer Fellow, Marion North Recipient and a Talawa Make Artist. She was on the creative choreographic team for the 2012 Olympics Opening Ceremony and is a member of the internationally acclaimed performance collective Hot Brown Honey.

Movement Director credits include: *The UK Drill Project* (Barbican), *Roundabout 22* (Paines Plough), *The Concrete Jungle Book* (The pleasance), *Kabul Goes Pop* (Brixton House), *Human Nurture* (Theatre Centre / Sheffield Theatre), *Athena* (The Yard Theatre), *Notes on Grief* (Manchester International Festival), *Rare Earth Mettle & Living Newspaper* (Royal Court), *Fuck You Pay Me* (Bunker), *Breakin' Convention* (Sadler's Wells), *Talawa TYPT* (Hackney Showrooms), *Boat* (BAC)

Director credits include: *Fierce Flow* (Hippodrome Birmingham), *Kind of Woman* (Camden People's), *Afroabelhas* (Roundhouse / British Council / Tempo Festival)

Assistant Director/Choreographer credits include: *Hive City Legacy* (Roundhouse, Home, Millennium), *Hive City Legacy; Dublin* (Dublin Fringe)

THEATRE CENTRE

THEATRE
CENTRE

Theatre Centre is a new writing, national touring theatre company, making bold, relevant shows with and for young people in schools, theatres, communities and digitally. We run Future Makers, a whole new way of collaborating with young people as artists, creative leaders and active citizens. It is central to all our work and is the key to how we unlock our young people-centred practice.

Future Makers embeds young people at the core of our work, bringing young people together with artists in democratised spaces to explore big, relevant issues. We listen actively and radically, using these insights to create shows, build relationships and deepen reach.

We commission new work from trailblazing writers in response to themes emerging from Future Makers, with the writer and young people collaborating to develop the work, and we take this work into schools and theatres across the UK. In 2021 we reached over 60,000 students in over 500 schools with the film of *Birds and Bees* by Charlie Josephine. In 2022 we toured Human Nurture by award-winning writer Ryan Calais Cameron to over sixty UK schools.

Theatre Centre has pioneered school touring since 1953 and is recognised as a ground-breaking force in young people-centred practice. We have long been a vital catalyst for youth leadership and creativity; nurturing writers at breakthrough points in their careers with commissions, dramaturgical support and access to other theatre makers.

In autumn 2023 we will celebrate seventy years of making work that changes lives.

www.theatre-centre.co.uk

Supported using public funding by

ARTS COUNCIL ENGLAND

LOTTERY FUNDED

SHEFFIELD THEATRES

SHEFF!ELD THEATRES

Sheffield Theatres is home to three theatres: the Crucible, the Sheffield landmark with a world-famous reputation; the Playhouse, an intimate, versatile space for getting closer to the action; and the gleaming Lyceum, the beautiful proscenium that hosts the best of the UK's touring shows. In November 2021, the Crucible and Playhouse theatres celebrated their fiftieth anniversary.

Having held the title 'Regional Theatre of the Year' on four separate occasions, Sheffield Theatres is the ticket to big names and local heroes, timeless treasures and new voices. Committed to investing in the creative leaders of the future, Sheffield Theatres' dedicated talent development hub, the Bank, opened in 2019 to support a new cohort of emerging theatre-makers every year.

Sheffield Theatres has a reputation for bold new work. The acclaimed *Life of Pi* began life at the Crucible, winning four awards at the 2019 UK Theatre Awards, 'Achievement in Technical Theatre' at the Stage Awards and 'Best New Play' at the WhatsOnStage Awards. The show opened in the West End in 2021, winning five Olivier Awards in 2022, and this year returns to Sheffield Theatres as part of a UK and Ireland tour. This success follows the phenomenal Sheffield musical *Everybody's Talking About Jamie* which also originated at the Crucible in 2017, before transferring to the West End, embarking on a UK tour and being turned into a feature film released simultaneously to 244 countries on Amazon Prime in September 2021.

Most recently, *Rock / Paper / Scissors*, three plays performed concurrently across the three theatres by a single cast, was staged as the centrepiece of Sheffield Theatres' fiftieth anniversary celebrations. Robert Hastie, Anthony Lau and Elin Schofield won Best Directors at the UK Theatre Awards 2022 for the ambitious trilogy. Concluding 2022, Sheffield Theatres, in co-production with the National Theatre and Various Productions, revived their multi-award-winning new musical *Standing at the Sky's Edge*. Originally staged in 2019, the hit show returned to the Crucible ahead of transferring to the National Theatre in February 2023.

Crucible Lyceum Playhouse: 55 Norfolk Street, Sheffield, S1 1DA

sheffieldtheatres.co.uk

Sheffield
City Council

Theatre Centre Team

Enterprise Manager	Hannah Austin
Marketing Manager	Rachel Bellman
Finance Director	David Lewis
Touring Producer	Amy Michaels
Strategic Development Partner	Moni Onojeruo
Programme & Admin Coordinator	Niamh Parker-Whitehead
Future Makers Producer	Ben Price
Executive Director & CEO	Emma Rees
Creative Associate	Monay Thomas
Artistic Director	Rob Watt

Sheffield Theatres Team

Chief Executive	Tom Bird
Deputy Chief Executive	Bookey Oshin
Artistic Director	Robert Hastie

Senior Management Team

Communications Director	Rachel Nutland
Producer	John Tomlinson
Associate Artistic Director	Anthony Lau
Customer Experience Director	Caroline Laurent
Operations Director	John Bates
HR Director	Andrea Ballantyne
Fundraising & Commercial Director	Elizabeth Barran
Finance Director	Kathy Gillibrand

Administration Team

HR Advisor	Lorna Tomlinson
HR Advisor	Lianne Froggatt
Assistant to Chief Executive & Artistic Director	Jackie Pass

Sales & Customer Experience Team

Front of House Manager	Debbie Smith
Deputy Front of House Manager	Jake Ross
Sales Managers	Kate Fisher, Louise Renwick
Sales & Customer Care Supervisor	Claire Fletcher
Access & Sales Supervisor	Paul Whitley
Sales & Groups Supervisor	Ian Caudwell
Sales Assistants	Rebecca Alldrick, Sue Cooper, Sally Field, Faye Hardaker, Charlotte Keyworth, Grace Sansom, Irene Stewart, Eleanor Towell, Katy Wainwright

Communications Team

Communications Manager	Oliver Eastwood
Communications Executive	Thomas Adcock
Media Officer	Carrie Askew
Communications Officer	Laura Hill
Multimedia Producer	Lucy Smith-Jones
Programmer	Helen Dobson

Producing Team

Consultant Producer	Matthew Byam Shaw
Company Manager	Andrew Wilcox
New Work Coordinator	Ruby Clarke
Talent Development Coordinator	Tommi Bryson
New Work Officer	Misha Duncan-Barry
Playright Mentor	Grace Gummer
Assistant Producer	James Ashfield
Trainee Producer	Miranda Debenham
Production Manager	Stephanie Balmforth
Stage Manager	Sarah Gentle
Deputy Stage Manager	Sarah Greenwood
Assistant Stage Manager	Rosalind Chappelle
Head of Wardrobe	Debbie Gamble
Deputy Heads of Wardrobe	Abi Nettleship, Sally Wilson
Wardrobe Assistants	Rose Jennings, Merle Richards-Wright, Sophie Sidhu
Wardrobe & Wig Mistress	Valerie Atkinson
Dressers	Gemma Anderson, Jess Atkinson, Lily Broadbent, Sophie Harvey, Abigail Hindley, Martha Lamb, Eleanor McBurnie, Jennifer Moore, Angela Platts, Katy Scott, Anouchka Santella, Amanda Thompson
Cutters	Silivia Devilly, Kate Harrison, Imogen Singer
Company in Residence	Utopia Theatre
Producer / Creative Director	Mojisola Elufowoju
Associate Company	Third Angel

Sheffield Theatres Trust Board

Theatre Centre would like to thank the following people:

Lewisham and Sheffield Future Makers, Lewisham Youth Theatre,
National Youth Theatre, Justin Kendal-Sadiq, Connie Fiddament,
Liliya Filippova, Noor Sobka, Hetty Hodgson, Hackney Empire,
Theatre Peckham, Dan Bates and Rob Hastie from Sheffield Theatres.

Zeena Rashid and National Drama, Alexander Perricone and Alliance
Berstein, Milk Presents and all the schools and young people from
across the UK who helped develop *Birds and Bees*.

Our Chair Titilola Dawudu and Trustees Aleksa Asme, Yamin Choudury,
Frazer Flintham, Gareth Hughes, David Luff, Rebecca Major,
Tayo Medupin, Vanessa Sauls.

To all the young people who helped during the many various R&Ds
– whose names include Alina Aleva, Zaki Ali, Dana Alpiste Hurtado,
Kyle Baker, Jamai Brown, Jasmine Brown, Jim Burke, Bradley Butler,
Myquacna Campbell, Alice Connolly, James Cottis, Ava Drew, Michael
Kodi Farrow, Christie Fewry, Ashley Gregory, Dela Ruta Hini, Tyler
Kinghorn, Georgie Lammiman, Zac Looker, Eoin McCaul, Michaela
Millians, Maisie Mouat, Abbie Neale, Gracie Oddie-James, Kai Roberts,
Anushka Samarasinghe, Vee Tames - thank you for your courage,
honesty and wit.

CHARACTERS

AARRON – 16, Black, male. Working class. Cool, cheeky and charming.

BILLY – 16, any race, AFAB nonbinary. Working class. An outsider who's secretly eager to play.

LEILAH – 16, Black, female. Working class. Razor-sharp wit, with a big, open heart.

MAISY – 16, white, female. Middle class. More childlike than the rest, but not to be underestimated.

AUTHOR'S NOTES

Stage directions are in italics and parentheses. Capital letters are used to suggest an emphasis on specific words.

A slash (/) indicates a fast run-on to the next line, almost an interruption.

A standalone period (.) indicates where someone should have a line but for some reason isn't speaking.

A slash with two periods (/..) indicates where a word can't be found and something physical happens instead. Perhaps it's a small, naturalistic gesture or perhaps a big, abstract movement. Each one is an invitation to express something physically.

THANKS

To Natalie Wilson for inspiring me to write passionately and politically for Theatre Centre. To Rob Watt for your radical kindness, fierce queer rage and big belly laughs. To Jonathan at the Agency for your persistent energy and enthusiasm. To Emma Rees, Ben Price and Niamh Parker-Whitehead at Theatre Centre, for organising and contracting with such care. To Lee Affen for your sound magic, to Bethany Wells for your wonderful design brain, and to Yami Löfvenberg for your movement brilliance.

To Ida, Regna, Narisha Lawson, Ike Bennett, E M Williams, Steven Atkinson, Xana, Archie Short and Damilola 'DK' Fashola for your brilliant work on the film and digital package version of *Birds And Bees*, all made during a global pandemic no less.

To all the young people who helped during the many various R&Ds – thank you for your courage, honesty and wit.

To my mum for teaching me some bits about the birds and the bees. To all the queer literature and lovers for filling in the gaps.

To my LGBTQ+ elders for showing me the way. To everyone who protested against Section 28. To everyone still healing that damage. To Sexplain, Tender, Stonewall, Gendered Intelligence and Mermaids for your tireless love and activism.

(We hear the play before we see it. It sounds sick. We walk in and see four actors making a track live, with loop pedals and microphones. It's exciting to watch. They smile and nod at us as we enter. No fourth wall. Full acknowledgment that this is a live piece of theatre. When everyone's ready, the actors dim the music and speak to us.)

BILLY. So, this is the situation. There's Cherrelle and Jack.

AARRON. He's my best mate.

LEILAH. She's mine.

MAISY. And they're like the school's hottest couple.

LEILAH. They're so cute together, honestly, it's unreal!

BILLY. And they're doing what young people in love do.

MAISY. Constant Instagram!

AARRON. Snapchat and TikTok for days!

LEILAH. Hashtag couple goals!

MAISY. Hashtag so in love!

BILLY. And I guess they must have been sending each other stuff, you know, videos and that. Private stuff, stuff that's *private* /

LEILAH. Until Jack made it public! Showing off to his mates!

AARRON. Hey, let's not speculate! We don't know exactly what happened /

LEILAH. Erm, I think we do!

MAISY. Yeah I think it's pretty obvious!

AARRON. I think that's unfair. Innocent until proven guilty and all that.

LEILAH. Nah cus /

BILLY. Anyway! However it happened, it got shared. Cherrelle's private video got shared.

MAISY. And in *seconds*, everyone's seen it!

EVERYONE. Everyone!

AARRON. And things kick off like, *so fast*!

MAISY. Yeah I was shocked!

LEILAH. Yeah cus like, this happens all the time /

MAISY. All the time!

LEILAH. But I don't think our parents even know, like, the extent of it.

AARRON. Yeah this is nothing new for us. But for some reason they heard about it /

BILLY. Parents, teachers, the school governors, the *police* /

AARRON. And it's all kicked off!

MAISY. Will Jack get arrested?

LEILAH. I dunno if it's even a crime?

BILLY. It is. But it's hard to prove he did it on purpose.

AARRON. He wouldn't have! It'd have been some stupid mistake /

LEILAH. She's not left her room for days!

MAISY. I wouldn't either.

LEILAH. Oh my god I'd die! I'd literally die!

AARRON. He's really upset too!

LEILAH. Good! So he should be!

BILLY. But the thing that's been really upsetting, is how the school's responded.

LEILAH. Yeah!

AARRON. Yeah it's a mess!

LEILAH. And now we're *stuck* here tryna pick up the pieces?!

AARRON. Tryna make sense of it all /

MAISY. And know what to do next.

LEILAH. I'm Leilah, by the way. This is my boyfriend.

AARRON. Aarron. Y'alright? And that's Maisy.

MAISY. Hi.

BILLY. And I'm Billy.

MAISY. We're in year eleven, about to do our GCSEs. I'm top of the year, and a prefect /

LEILAH. Oh my God /

AARRON. No one cares Maisy /

MAISY. I do /

LEILAH. Anyway!

BILLY. Yeah, so that's that. Intro done! You're all caught up with the backstory, so now we can get started. Scene One. Aarron's alone. Leilah enters.

> (*Music stops, lights shift.* **BILLY** *and* **MAISY** *sit down at the side of the stage and watch the scene.* **LEILAH** *and* **AARRON** *see each other.* **LEILAH** *is unimpressed.*)

AARRON. Ah! Don't look at me like that!

LEILAH. Don't speak to me!

AARRON. Babes!

LEILAH. Don't 'babes' me!

AARRON. Ah come on! It's not my fault I /

LEILAH. Whose fault is it then Aarron?! Not yours, no, 'course not! Cus you *never* take responsibility!

AARRON. Hang on, I /

LEILAH. You *avoid* speaking to me /

AARRON. I was try/

LEILAH. About *anything* serious, *anything* even slightly deep, at all /

AARRON. I'm trying to /

LEILAH. We're meant to be in a relationship? And you can't even speak to me /

AARRON. Yeah but, I'm try/

LEILAH. About how you're feeling? That's *basic*! You can't honestly connect with me /

AARRON. *I was trying to!*

LEILAH. In *assembly*?! In the Special Assembly they're holding because our best friends are in trouble, *that's* the time you choose? Oh yeah nice one babes! Perfect timing! Wonderful! *What is wrong with you?!*

AARRON. Look, I didn't /

LEILAH. Now we're stuck in *here* when I should be seeing Cherrelle!

AARRON. I know, I /

LEILAH. And *you* should be seeing Jack, to work out what the hell he's been playing at /

AARRON. I /

LEILAH. Have you spoken to Jack?

AARRON. No I /

LEILAH. Why not?! You're always together.

AARRON. His mum won't let anyone /

LEILAH. Were you there when he did it?

AARRON. What?! No! I /

LEILAH. I swear down Aarron, if you had *anything* to do with /

AARRON. I didn't! I swear! I had no idea that Jack would do that! It's not like him, he's not /

LEILAH. Did you delete the ones I sent you?

AARRON. Yes!

LEILAH. All of them?

AARRON. Yes! I swear! ...Even the really hot ones /

LEILAH. Aarron!

AARRON. What?

> (*He dances his way over to her, cheeky and charming. She pouts, trying not to laugh, but he's actually really funny.*)

Ah look, come on. You know I'm not like that. I wouldn't do that to you!

LEILAH. (*Softer.*) No, you just get me in trouble.

AARRON. Nah, nah come now. You know that wasn't my /

LEILAH. Fault? Oh my gosh! My *best friend* needs me, and I'm stuck in here, with you. And you're tryna tell me it's *not* your fault?! Seriously?!

AARRON. It's not! I /

LEILAH. Say that again! I dare you! Try and duck the blame again Aarron, I *dare* you!

AARRON. Babes /

LEILAH. Don't 'babes' me! Don't speak to me!

(**LEILAH** *gets her phone out and scrolls furiously.* **MAISY** *enters.* **LEILAH** *and* **AARRON** *stop dead.*)

AARRON & LEILAH. Maisy?!

AARRON. Wot are *you* doin' *here*?!

LEILAH. You're *never* in trouble!

MAISY. I know.

(**MAISY** *puts her bags down, and they stare at her.*)

AARRON. Nah! Nah never!

MAISY. Apparently so. Sitting next to you Aarron, as you disrupt assembly /

AARRON. Nah that wasn't /

MAISY. Is apparently crime enough! And now I've got to waste precious studying time being here with you?

LEILAH. Oh charming!

MAISY. Sir said we've got to work together to have an *honest* discussion /

AARRON. Yeah we know!

MAISY. And to write a formal apology /

AARRON. For what?!

MAISY. That we present to the year /

LEILAH. Nah /

MAISY. In tomorrow morning's assembly /

LEILAH. Nah. Nah I'm not doing that! No way!

MAISY. Okay. So, Aarron, let's start with /

AARRON. Yeah I ain't apologising for shit!

MAISY. Oh wow, what a fantastic attitude! That's so helpful for us! Thank you Aarron, thank you so much.

LEILAH. Sarcasm ain't clever you know. It's just rude.

MAISY. Well we're in enough trouble as it is! Oh my god. I can't believe *I'm* in trouble, I'm *never* in trouble, I'm a *Prefect*!

LEILAH. And you're late.

MAISY. What?

LEILAH. You're late. So that's more trouble. Double trouble.

> (**MAISY** *clenches her fists and stares at* **LEILAH**, *who backs away, amused.*)

MAISY. I, am, not, *late*! I am *never* late!

LEILAH. Okay!

> (**AARRON** *chuckles and* **MAISY** *glares at him.*)

MAISY. I was in the office actually, stating my case.

AARRON. *(Laughs.)* Case!

MAISY. I've spent *all day* trying to explain to them that I don't deserve to be here. I've *never* been in trouble. I've had a *clean* slate, for *five*, *years*! Until today! Until *you* decided to /

AARRON. It wasn't *my* fault!

LEILAH. Wow!

MAISY. You interrupted the *Headmaster's* speech?! What were you thinking?!

AARRON. They shouldn't have been bangin' on like that! A *'special assembly'*? You jokin'?! Like that's gonna solve anythin'?

MAISY. Well, what is it exactly that *you* would /

AARRON. I should have known it'd be dead. As *soon* as they announced it. As *soon* as they said they were doing a /

AARRON & LEILAH. *'Special Assembly'!*

AARRON. To discuss the /

AARRON & LEILAH. *'Incident'!*

AARRON. Dead! So dead!

MAISY. I don't understand.

LEILAH. There wasn't exactly much *discussion*, was there? More of a one-way conversation. A monologue, if you like.

AARRON. Haha yeah! *'Two of our students have let everyone down!'*

MAISY. Yes, okay yes, but I'm sure that they were just trying to /

LEILAH. And it was soooo long?! He uses like fifty *thousand* words when like, one or two would do?!

AARRON. Proper pointing the finger.

MAISY. That's, that's not *quite*, what was /

LEILAH. Why are you defending them?!

MAISY. I'm not! I'm not, I'm just /

AARRON. Nah! Nah! What happened in there was *madness*!

LEILAH. Lecturing us?

AARRON. Being all like, *patronising* and shit?

LEILAH. So patronising! Talking to us like we're stupid? Like we're literally children?

AARRON. *'You shouldn't be sexting!'*

LEILAH. Urgh! I literally gagged when Mr Thompkins said that!

AARRON. *'Sending nudes is very, very dangerous!'*

LEILAH. Gross!

MAISY. Well, it is.

AARRON. Wot?

MAISY. It is, dangerous.

(**LEILAH** *and* **AARRON** *laugh at her.*)

LEILAH. Wow! Okay?! This is 2023 babes! We're not like some Victorian old people!

MAISY. Yeah, but /..

LEILAH. What?

MAISY. .

LEILAH. What?!

MAISY. It's just, pretty stupid.

LEILAH. Oh my gosh?! You did *not* just call my best friend stupid?!

MAISY. No! I'm, I just, *sexting*, is stupid? Is, sometimes /

LEILAH. Oh my gosh?!

AARRON. Mais, do yourself a favour and shut up man!

LEILAH. Cherrelle is like *literally* my sister?!

MAISY. I know! I mean /

AARRON. Jack's my best mate!

MAISY. Yeah! I know, I mean, I know that she /

LEILAH. No you don't. You don't know what happened!

MAISY. No, no I don't know, *all* the details /

LEILAH. No! So mind your own business!

MAISY. I'm just saying /

LEILAH. Well don't!

MAISY. The *situation* is stupid. I'm just saying that /

AARRON. For a clever girl you sound like an idiot!

MAISY. I just. I actually think the school is handling it really well /

LEILAH. Wow!

MAISY. I mean it's delicate isn't it?

AARRON. Trust you to take their side!

MAISY. There are no sides! They're trying to protect us!

AARRON. Yeah sure!

MAISY. Look, the ones to blame here are Cherrelle and Jack, not the school.

LEILAH & AARRON. What?!

MAISY. Well, the truth is we wouldn't have even *been* in assembly, if they hadn't done it. We wouldn't be *here* now /

LEILAH. If *Aarron* hadn't kicked off we wouldn't!

AARRON. I didn't 'kick off'! I said *one* word!

MAISY. 'For fuckssake' is at least two.

AARRON. Woteva.

MAISY. Oh my god, we're in so much trouble! I knew I shouldn't have sat near you. I just *knew* it!

LEILAH. And like, I was a bit proud of you babes I'm not gonna lie, but also like, *pick your moment* you know?! Now's *really* not the time to be a hero.

AARRON. I wasn't being a hero.

LEILAH. So what were you doing?

AARRON. Tryna get *your* attention! You kept ignoring me?!

LEILAH. Oh. *(On mic.)* And *why* was I ignoring you Aarron? Wanna talk about that?

AARRON. Not really.

MAISY. It was obvious *I* wasn't being disruptive. I mean, as if I'd *ever* interrupt /

LEILAH. *(On mic.)* No! 'Course not! Cus you *never* wanna talk about /

AARRON. *(On mic.)* You *always* wanna talk about *every*, *little*, *thing*!

LEILAH. *(On mic.)* Oh my gosh /

AARRON. *(On mic.)* Over and *over*! Making *everything* such a big deal?!

LEILAH. *(On mic.)* Wow!

MAISY. This will be on my records! It's just *so unfair*! I've been working *so hard*! Why should I be punished because you couldn't /

AARRON. Alright Mais. Can you just shut up a minute /

MAISY. No it's not alright! We've got *exams* coming up! I should be studying right, *now*! But instead I'm in *here*, with *you*, all because some of your friends couldn't keep their clothes on in front of a camera /

LEILAH. Woah, hang on /

MAISY. Our *final exams*?! I am *not failing* because of *you*!

AARRON. Oh come on Mais, you're not gonna fail!

MAISY. You're right, I'm not! Just need to stay *focused*. Work *hard*, stay *focused*, work hard, stay focused, work hard, stay /

AARRON. Are you crying?!

MAISY. No!

AARRON. You are!

MAISY. I'm not!

LEILAH. Wow!

AARRON. You need to chill out, seriously, meditate or some shit. Like yoga, try yoga yeah? Do that humming thing like, ommmmmmmm!

> *(He laughs at himself. No one else laughs.)*

Okay!

LEILAH. Look, none of us wanna be here Maisy, it's not just you.

AARRON. Yeah I'm meant to be at training right now.

LEILAH. I'm meant to be seeing Cherrelle!

AARRON. We've got tryouts next week.

LEILAH. She really needs me!

AARRON. This could be my Big Chance!

LEILAH. And I'm not there for her! And I can't even message her because her mum's taken her stupid phone!

AARRON. I scored twelve goals last season, so I should be /

LEILAH. Can you shut up about football?!

AARRON. Erm, no. *(Big grin.)* I can't. And I don't want to.

> *(He does a mic-drop dance, making himself laugh.* **MAISY** *and* **LEILAH** *are not impressed.)*

LEILAH. You're a joke!

AARRON. *What* is your problem /

LEILAH. There's more *important things* going on Aarron!

AARRON. Okay!

LEILAH. But you don't wanna talk about them?! You don't wanna talk about anything serious, ever!

AARRON. Serious serious!

LEILAH. *All* you wanna talk about is *football*, and *sex*!

AARRON. Well, yeah.

LEILAH. Oh, get out my face!

AARRON. Babes, come on /

LEILAH. Oh my gosh! You're so stupid! You're actually so stupid!

AARRON. *(Quietly.)* Don't.

LEILAH. What?

AARRON. *(Quietly.)* Don't call me that.

LEILAH. Well then don't act like it Aarron, you're embarrassing yourself.

AARRON. Fine. I'm goin'.

> (**AARRON** *picks up his bag and moves towards the door.*)

MAISY. You can't!

AARRON. Watch me!

LEILAH. Aarron, you actually can't.

AARRON. Nah nah nah I'm done! I'm *done*!

> (**AARRON** *paces, but there's nowhere to go. He eventually returns to his position.*)

LEILAH. Told you. We can't leave until we've all been honest. Dem's da rules.

> (**LEILAH** *flicks her hair, smug.* **AARRON** *glares at her.* **LEILAH** *sticks her tongue out and scrolls on her phone.* **BILLY** *suddenly calls out from the side of the stage.*)

BILLY. Go on then.

LEILAH. Go on what?

BILLY. Be honest. Be real. And no, I don't mean the app.

> (**LEILAH** *shoves her phone aside and glares at* **BILLY**.)

LEILAH. What are you on about /

BILLY. You've obviously got somethin' to say, you always do. And if we've all gotta be honest, *all* includes you.

LEILAH. You're not even in the scene yet. Why you getting involved?

MAISY. *(Staring wide-eyed at the audience.)* Er, guys, can we please stick to the script?

AARRON. They're right though. Go on Leilah, get honest. Say something /

LEILAH. Oh, I'm always honest! I say it how it is, always have, always will. I wear my heart on my sleeve and I /

BILLY. Nah nah nah come on! What's really going on? Under all that front.

AARRON. Yeah, take off the armour and be true for a second. Come on! Speak truth!

LEILAH. .

AARRON. Thought so. Not just me that finds it hard eh?

LEILAH. Nah it's just that I don't wanna speak if you're not listening!

AARRON. I'm listening!

LEILAH. No you ain't!

AARRON. Oh my God!

MAISY. Look, sir said /

LEILAH. *(Mimicking.)* Sir said!

MAISY. We've got to have an honest discussion, as a group /

AARRON. No thanks!

MAISY. What?

AARRON. Nah, I'm alright.

LEILAH. You see, always avoiding open communi/

AARRON. I'm not avoiding, I just don't want to.

MAISY. Well we have to! And as soon as we've done it we can leave.

AARRON. Yeah great okay, what do you want me to say?

MAISY. What?

AARRON. Tell me what you want me to say and I'll say it. So we can go.

MAISY. You can't fast-forward the /

AARRON. Why not?

LEILAH. You're ridiculous!

MAISY. Look sir said /

AARRON. Sir chats shit!

> (**LEILAH** *tries not to laugh.* **AARRON** *smiles at her.*)

MAISY. Very funny. But we're actually in enough Trouble as it is. And the quickest way out of here, is by working together, as a Team.

LEILAH. A team? Seriously, what a joke! I mean, *you*, and *me*?! We're not exactly /

MAISY. What?

LEILAH. Compatible.

MAISY. Ooh, is that the longest word you know?

> (**AARRON** *laughs with* **MAISY**.)

LEILAH. Listen hun, I suggest you sort all of *(Gestures to* **MAISY**'s *appearance.)* this, out, before you ever speak to me again. Yeah?

MAISY. .

AARRON. Babes /

LEILAH. Don't speak to me.

MAISY. Look, I've already written some points down that we could say. Just to speed things up. So we just need to /

AARRON. When?! Assembly was this *morning*?

MAISY. At lunch.

AARRON. Wow! Do you ever just like, have fun?

　　　　　*(***LEILAH** *laughs.)*

MAISY. Do you understand how *serious* this is?!

AARRON. Okay!

MAISY. We've got to work together. If we don't then /

AARRON. Wot?

MAISY. Then we'll have failed, and I'll be a failure! Even though I'm a prefect, and my behaviour has been immaculate for *five years*, and I've given my education my everything, this will be a mark on my record! Which will affect my UCAS application, which will affect whether I can get into university which will affect my career which will affect the rest of my entire life! And I'll end up working in Primark!

LEILAH. What's wrong with working in Primark?

AARRON. Leilah works in Primark.

MAISY. No offence! It's just, *not* my dream! And *I* have to work for *my* dreams! *Every day!*

LEILAH. Wow! Are you always this uptight?

AARRON. Haha! Yeah, she is!

MAISY. Look, I just need you to read it, and agree with it, then we can all go, can you do that, please?

LEILAH. Looks exhausting, honestly!

AARRON. Yeah!

LEILAH. No wonder no one likes you.

MAISY. Look, you might want to mess about, and focus on your social life, and ruin your education, but some of us want to *work*. Some of us want to get the grades we *deserve*, so we go to Uni and get Good jobs and travel the World. And not just stay here, and get pregnant like Some Girls Do, stay glued to Instagram and gossip, to avoid admitting they're stuck in some *Shitty Little Miserable Life*!

> *(Silence.* **LEILAH** *launches at* **MAISY.** **AARRON** *holds* **LEILAH** *back.* **BILLY** *speaks into a microphone from the side of the stage, which distracts* **LEILAH.***)*

BILLY. Ah yes. This is a classic example of conflict in storytelling. The two antagonists go head to head, whilst the fool attempts to intervene.

AARRON. Er, who you calling a fool?

BILLY. This conflict will escalate until something diffuses it. Which makes *this* moment the *perfect* opportunity to introduce a *gorgeous* new character.

> *(***BILLY** *stands.)*

Ta-dah!

> *(***BILLY** *enters.* **MAISY** *runs behind* **BILLY** *and uses them for cover.)*

MAISY. Oh thank God! Help! She's lost it!

LEILAH. You better watch yourself Maisy /

AARRON. Leilah /

LEILAH. Keep your mouth shut! I mean it!

AARRON. Leilah!

LEILAH. Wot?!

AARRON. What the hell?! Literally never seen you like this /

LEILAH. Well she winds me up!

AARRON. Okay! Just chill babes! Seriously. She ain't worth it.

> (**LEILAH** *sulks, scrolling on her phone.* **MAISY**
> *cowers, as far away from* **LEILAH** *as possible.*
> **AARRON** *stands between them.* **BILLY** *looks at*
> *them all.*)

BILLY. Why you here?

> (**AARRON** *stares at* **BILLY**, *unsure what to*
> *make of them.*)

LEILAH. Erm, weren't you in assembly?

BILLY. No.

LEILAH. Oh.

BILLY. .

LEILAH. How comes?

BILLY. I have therapy on Monday mornings.

LEILAH. Right.

> (*No one knows what to do with this information.*
> **BILLY** *shrugs.* **AARRON** *is still staring at* **BILLY**.)

MAISY. We're all stuck here, because we sat next to Aarron /

AARRON. Nah /

MAISY. Who disrupted today's assembly /

AARRON. Nah /

LEILAH. The 'Special Assembly', about Jack and Cherrelle.

BILLY. Who's Jack and Cherrelle?

AARRON, MAISY & LEILAH. *What?!*

BILLY. I'm joking! I know who they are. Everyone does. I didn't watch the video. I saw it but I didn't watch it.

LEILAH. .

BILLY. I saw the photos though. Someone posted them yesterday, and I saw them before I could even look away. She's quite the little poser! She *really* shouldn't have /

LEILAH. Wot?!

BILLY. Let her face be in them. School-girl error! And Jack shouldn't have shared them. But I guess no one's teaching us this stuff so *(Shrugs.)*

LEILAH. Why you here?

BILLY. 'Back-chatting' a teacher.

LEILAH. Which teacher?

BILLY. Mrs Hadley.

AARRON & LEILAH. Ooooh!

(**AARRON** *and* **LEILAH** *shudder, then laugh.*)

LEILAH. You're brave!

BILLY. Nah, I'm tired. PSHE? What a load of shit!

MAISY. What did you say?

BILLY. I asked about queer sex.

LEILAH. *(Laughing.)* What?!

BILLY. I asked her if like, the entire syllabus was gonna reinforce such heteronormative, patriarchal and frankly outdated opinions. Don't think she knew the answer. But it was when I asked about strap-ons that she went proper mental!

> (**LEILAH** *laughs.* **MAISY** *blushes.* **AARRON** *looks confused.* **LEILAH** *gets her phone out and uses the selfie-camera to check her appearance.* **BILLY** *watches her, and she enjoys being watched.* **AARRON** *sees this spark between* **BILLY** *and* **LEILAH** *and gets territorial.*)

AARRON. You look fit babes.

LEILAH. No I don't! I look a right mess.

AARRON. Never! Fitty 24/7.

LEILAH. Shuttup!

> (**LEILAH** *enjoys the compliment.* **AARRON** *sits next to her and they take selfies together.* **MAISY** *and* **BILLY** *try not to watch.* **LEILAH** *suddenly turns around to take a Snapchat of the whole room.*)

Rebels club!

MAISY. *(Covering her face.)* No no NO! DON'T!

AARRON. Woah! Chill Maisy it's just /

MAISY. Please don't post that! Seriously! *Please* don't post that!

LEILAH. Alright! Chill out!

MAISY. If my dad sees that he'll go mental!

LEILAH. How's your dad gonna /

MAISY. Please! You dunno what he's like!

LEILAH. Okay okay I'll delete it!

MAISY. .

BILLY. My dad's strict too.

MAISY. *(Quietly.)* It's just because he cares. Says I've got Potential, and, he doesn't want to see me waste it.

> (**AARRON** *and* **LEILAH** *stifle a laugh.* **MAISY** *glares at them.)*

BILLY. He must be really proud of you.

MAISY. .

AARRON. Wish I had *potential*.

> (**LEILAH** *laughs.* **MAISY***'s fists clench.* **BILLY** *watches her.)*

MAISY. *(Under her breath.)* Work hard stay focused work hard stay focused /

LEILAH. *(To* **AARRON**.*)* Oh babes I love that one of us!

MAISY. *(Under her breath.)* Work hard stay focused work hard /

LEILAH. *(To* **AARRON**.*)* We look fit.

MAISY. *(Suddenly turning to* **LEILAH**.*)* Promise you deleted it?

LEILAH. Yes!

MAISY. Please. Don't post it /

LEILAH. I won't!

BILLY. *(Calmly.)* Yeah don't, it's not cool.

> (**LEILAH** *pouts but puts her phone away.* **MAISY** *beams at* **BILLY**, *who turns away from her, uninterested.)*

MAISY. Billy? It is Billy, right?

BILLY. Yup.

MAISY. Cool! I'm Maisy. I'm a Prefect.

BILLY. I know.

MAISY.   Cool! Well, Billy, sir said we've got to work together. To have an *honest* discussion, about recent events. And then we have to present our points, along with an apology, to the year, tomorrow morning in assembly /

LEILAH. I'm not doing that! I told you /

MAISY. Because Aarron disrupted today's /

AARRON. Oh yeah blame it all on me /

MAISY. And I've written a draft! That could do with an outside eye.

LEILAH. Hang on, you haven't even shown *us* yet! Not interested in *our* opinion on it?

MAISY. I, I just thought we /

AARRON. You cheatin' Maisy?!

MAISY. No!

AARRON. Oooooh!

> (*He does a silly dance.*)

Cheeky-cheat-cheat! Cheeky-cheat-cheat!

MAISY. No I'm not /

AARRON. Cheeky-cheat-ahhhh!

> (**LEILAH** *laughs.*)

MAISY. No! I don't, *cheat*, ever. I just thought she might be interested in /

BILLY. They.

MAISY. What?

BILLY. My pronouns are they/them.

MAISY. (*Not understanding.*) Right. Erm, can I read it to you?

BILLY. Sure.

LEILAH. I'll read it. *(She snatches it off* **MAISY** *and starts reading.)* Recent events surrounding fellow students Jack and Cherrelle have made it clear that we need a clamp down on sexting.

AARRON. 'Clamp down'?

LEILAH. *(Reading.)* Before any more students make foolish mistakes. *(Looks up.)* You calling Cherrelle a fool?

MAISY. No, no I /

LEILAH. I'm not saying this! Cherrelle's my mate.

*(***AARRON*** grabs the speech off* **LEILAH**.*)*

MAISY. I know she's your /

LEILAH. I'm not making out like it's *her* fault!

AARRON. *(Reading.)* Whilst we are all aware that sex is something that happens between man and wife, the youth of today have easy access to the internet /

LEILAH. No shit /

AARRON. Which is accelerating their exposure to sexual imagery and media. *(Looks up.)* So that's porn yeah?

LEILAH. This is so dumb!

*(***MAISY*** grabs it back.)*

MAISY. *(Reading.)* Whilst sexual behaviour, between man and wife, is of course natural. Technology is introducing an *unnatural* acceleration of sexuality /

BILLY. Erm, gonna have to stop you there!

MAISY. What?

BILLY. It's a bit, reductionist.

MAISY. Which bit?

BILLY. Erm. All of it?

> (**LEILAH** *laughs.* **AARRON** *frowns, jealous.*)

AARRON. Reductionist? *(Does a robot dance.)* Re-duck, re-re-re, re-duck!

> (**AARRON** *laughs at himself, but no one joins in, and he sulks.*)

MAISY. I'm following the suggested guidelines from the Government's curriculum!

BILLY. Exactly.

MAISY. What do you want me to do?

BILLY. Think for yourself?

> (**LEILAH** *laughs with* **BILLY**. **AARRON** *frowns.* **MAISY** *blushes, furious.*)

AARRON. Babes?

LEILAH. *(Not looking at him.)* Yeah?

AARRON. Come here a minute.

LEILAH. *(Not looking at him.)* Yeah.

BILLY. Look, I didn't mean to offend you.

MAISY. I'm not offended!

BILLY. Cool! It's just, your choice of language, yeah? Like, around gender for example. It's not inclusive of all people. And your ideas on /

MAISY. All people?

BILLY. 'Man and wife'?

LEILAH. Yeah you don't have to be *married* to have sex Maisy /

MAISY. I know! Of course I know that! I'm a feminist! My mum educated me in women's rights from a *really* young age. I just meant /

AARRON. Yeah your mum's fit! I saw her in town, and was like, oh my days! Maisy's *mum*!

LEILAH. Shuttup Aarron!

MAISY. Yes, please, that's really inappropriate!

LEILAH. Oi yeah, I *hate* how people say '*man and wife*'! Like, like he owns her or some shit?

BILLY. Like she hasn't got her own agency?

LEILAH. Yeah!

BILLY. Or sexuality?

LEILAH. Yeah! And they only ever talk about penises!

AARRON. Yeah course! Cus man's gotta /

LEILAH. Shuttup Aarron! Like, '*Here's how a baby is made.*' But, what if you don't want a baby? What if you just wanna have sex cus it feels good?

MAISY. I, I don't think that's /

BILLY. Exactly! A clitoris is an organ designed solely for pleasure.

LEILAH. Oh my gosh yes! They should do classes on that!

BILLY. Help men to find them.

LEILAH. Hahaha exactly!

AARRON. *(Frowning.)* Wot?

LEILAH. Seriously though. '*Man and wife*'? Nah. You don't have to be a *man* to like sex.

BILLY. Or a woman. You don't have to subscribe to the gender binary at all, ya get me?

LEILAH. Yes!

MAISY. .

BILLY. You look confused.

MAISY. No! No I'm /.. I'm just /..

BILLY. I'm not a girl, or a boy, and I'm having great sex. Really great.

> (**LEILAH** *can't help but smile at* **BILLY**. **AARRON** *glares.* **MAISY** *is confused.*)

MAISY. What? With *who*?!

BILLY. Ah, nah, we don't kiss and tell.

> (**BILLY** *winks.* **LEILAH** *laughs.* **AARRON** *explodes.*)

AARRON. Wot d'you mean you're not a girl?!

BILLY. I'm not.

AARRON. Right. So you're a boy?

LEILAH. Aarron.

AARRON. So you're a boy yeah?

BILLY. No.

AARRON. No?!

LEILAH. Aarron /

AARRON. Nah I'm interested! So you're not a boy, and you're not a girl? Then what are you, a freak?

BILLY. Okaaaaa/

LEILAH. Aarron /

AARRON. That what you are? Little freak?

> (*He gets right up in* **BILLY**'s *face.* **BILLY** *stares at the floor.*)

You listening to me? Freak?

LEILAH. Aarron, stop it!

> (**BILLY**'s *body suddenly glitches. No one else notices, but their body violently jerks and*

twists. Repetitive movements, suspended in air, caught in angular shapes. It's urgent and animal, like something deep inside of them is trying to get out. This moment is supported by lights and sound. Then, as fast as it came, it's gone, ignored, like it didn't even happen. **BILLY** *is still again, staring at the floor.)*

AARRON. You listening to me? Freak?

LEILAH. Aarron, stop it!

AARRON. I'm just asking!

LEILAH. No you're being a dick!

(**LEILAH** *pulls* **AARRON** *away. Awkward silence.)*

MAISY. Okay, well, we have not got much time, and we've *got* to work on this, *together*. This *has* to be good. We just need to apologise and then they'll /

LEILAH. For what? We've got nothing to apologise for /

MAISY. *(Ignoring her.)* Here Aarron, you try reading this bit.

AARRON. Nah. I ain't saying that shit you wrote before.

MAISY. Come on!

AARRON. No.

MAISY. We just have to do it *once*. Say what they wanna hear, play the system.

BILLY. Careful it ain't playing you.

MAISY. *(Ignoring* **BILLY***.)* Just once! Get it over and done with, and then we can /

AARRON. No. No way.

MAISY. We *have* to!

LEILAH. I'll re-write it.

MAISY. Hahaha! Oh, are you being serious?

>   (**LEILAH***'s fists clench.*)

No offence. But I'm clearly the strongest writer in the group, so /

AARRON. Go on then.

MAISY. Okay, okay, so /..

>   (*She re-reads the essay.* **LEILAH** *sighs loudly.* **MAISY** *tries not to react.*)

Okay, I could change *'man and wife'* to *'men and women'*.

>   (**LEILAH** *snorts.* **MAISY** *glares at her.* **BILLY** *lifts their head to say something, but then changes their mind.*)

Or actually, *'women, and men'*.

LEILAH. *(Sarcastic.)* Oooh! You're so radical!

MAISY. *(Suddenly turning on* **LEILAH**.*)* Yeah, because sexting is *really* radical isn't it?

LEILAH. What?

MAISY. It's *so* clever isn't it? So empowered! Not attention seeking at all.

>   (**LEILAH***'s fists clench.*)

It's just *so* cool /

AARRON. Maisy /

MAISY. To be caught exposing your body /

AARRON. Mais/

MAISY. In the desperate attempt to be liked.

>   (**LEILAH***'s body suddenly glitches, violent and frantic. Unseen by* **MAISY** *and* **AARRON**, *but*

watched carefully by **BILLY**. **LEILAH***'s body thrashes and twists and turns. Her body spits out the phrase 'can't you see?' but in stops and starts, interrupted by something, distorted and disturbed.)*

LEILAH.   *C-c-c-ccan't-c-c-c-can't-y-y-y-y-can't y-can't y-can't y-can't you-can't you-can't you-can't you-can't yous-can't yous-can't yous-can't yousee-can't you see?!*

>*(This moment is supported by lights and sound.* **LEILAH** *suddenly sees that* **BILLY** *can see her glitch, and freezes. We snap back to reality.)*

MAISY. It's just *so* cool /

AARRON. Maisy /

MAISY. To be caught exposing your body /

AARRON. Mais/

MAISY. In the desperate attempt to be liked.

LEILAH. .

AARRON. You need to learn to shut up, seriously.

MAISY. .

BILLY. You never done it?

MAISY. Done what?

BILLY. Sent nudes.

MAISY. No!

AARRON. Maisy'd never do such a thing!

LEILAH. Maisy's never been laid.

AARRON. Leilah!

LEILAH. What?! Nah I'm sorry but she's judging *me*, when she ain't got a clue what she's talking about!

AARRON. It's okay Maisy. Being a Virgin is cool. Some men prefer it, you know?

LEILAH. Shut up Aarron!

(**MAISY** *blushes.*)

BILLY. It is actually cool. It's your body, your choice.

MAISY. Yes! Thank you I know, I /.. My *choice* to, delay, becoming sexually active, is actually in pursuit of my academic focus.

BILLY. Sure.

MAISY. But even if I was, active, I wouldn't put myself in such a vulnerable position.

BILLY. Right.

MAISY. This constant sexual objectification of women's bodies is very tiring.

BILLY. Very!

MAISY. And ultimately, it's just, not very /..

LEILAH. Wot? Ladylike?

MAISY. Feminist.

BILLY. Ah.

AARRON. Maisy *loves* a bit of feminism.

LEILAH. That right?

AARRON. Oh yeah! Never shuts up about it. You're a feminist ain't ya Mais/

MAISY. Proudly.

AARRON. See. Proper burn her bra and that.

MAISY. That's not what it means.

LEILAH. That's interesting.

MAISY. Is it?

LEILAH. Yeah.

MAISY. .

LEILAH. Kinda got me wondering though. Seems a bit, narrow, your feminism.

MAISY. What are you talking about?

LEILAH. Intersectionality.

>   (**BILLY** *snorts a laugh.*)

MAISY. *(Confused.)* What?

AARRON. Uh-oh! Clever Maisy don't know somethin'?!

LEILAH. Every day's a school day!

MAISY. *(Fists clenched.)* That's not a word.

AARRON. Inter-sexy what?

LEILAH.   Intersectionality. Kimberlé Crenshaw. 1989. Google it, you might learn somethin'.

>   (**MAISY** *pauses before rushing to google on her phone.* **LEILAH** *pouts.* **BILLY** *stifles a giggle. The pressure builds in* **MAISY**.*)*

AARRON. Inter-sexy-sexy! My girl's sexy-sexy!

LEILAH. Shuttup /

AARRON. Okay!

>   (**MAISY** *glitches, unseen by* **LEILAH** *and* **AARRON**, *but watched carefully by* **BILLY**. **MAISY** *spins and sees* **BILLY** *watching and freezes.*)

Inter-sexy-sexy! My girl's sexy-sexy!

LEILAH. Shuttup /

AARRON. Okay!

LEILAH. Some women, right, they *claim* to be feminist, when actually they ain't got a clue. Oh no, they're ignorant. They're privileged, and they sit there judging others /

MAISY. *You* judge *me*!

LEILAH. You clearly thought I was dumb, didn't you? And why's that? Cus I'm gorgeous?

AARRON. Eyyyy!

LEILAH. Cus I'm Black?

AARRON. Ohhhh!

MAISY. No, that's not what /

LEILAH. Cus my family is less economically privileged than yours?

MAISY. You don't know about my /

AARRON. Oh come on Maisy, we've all seen your dad's car.

BILLY. Yeah, if you're middle class, just own it.

AARRON. Innit! I would!

LEILAH. You thought I was dumb? Big mistake.

AARRON. Huge! Cus actually you're a smart, talented, sexy queen that I am blessed to call my own.

LEILAH. Thanks babes.

(*They kiss.* **MAISY** *tries again.*)

MAISY. I'm not saying it's *dumb* to take photos. Just that, in a patriarchal society, it *is* a vulnerable position to put yourself in. And with the *constant* sexual objectification of women's bodies in mass media, surely a more *feminist* stance would be to *avoid* taking nude photos.

AARRON. (*Laughs.*) Nude!

BILLY. That's a valid argument.

LEILAH. Nah! If a girl wants to take photos, to *express* herself, then that's her right!

MAISY. Fine! But she shouldn't be surprised when they get spread /

LEILAH. That wasn't her fault!

MAISY. If she didn't want them *seen* she shouldn't have taken them!

LEILAH. If she didn't wanna get raped she shouldn't have worn that short skirt?

MAISY. That's not what I'm saying /

LEILAH. No?

MAISY. It's not the same argument /

LEILAH. Yes it is! It's about *consent* /

MAISY. No! You're twisting the /

LEILAH. Cherrelle *trusted* him! It was a *private* conversation!

MAISY. Yeah, well, it's public now.

LEILAH. Yeah! Because of Jack! Oh my god! I literally hate him so much!

AARRON. Oi he's my bro!

LEILAH. He's a total prick!

AARRON. Wotever.

LEILAH. Urgh! I *hate* boys! Seriously! They say all these lovely things but actually /.. They're literally all the same. I mean, I can't *believe* he did that?! And of course *she's* being punished more than him!

AARRON. They're *both* expelled?

LEILAH. Yeah but she's getting more shit for it!

AARRON. No she's not!

LEILAH. Everyone's blaming her!

AARRON. Everyone's blaming *him*!

LEILAH. No Aarron, you don't understand!

> (**AARRON** *glitches slightly, unseen by everyone but* **BILLY**. **LEILAH** *continues talking over* **AARRON***'s glitch.*)

It's different for women. Cherrelle can't leave the house! *Constant* online abuse?! The stuff they're calling her? It's proper damaging! While, all the time, Jack gets congratulated?!

> (**AARRON** *glitches again.*)

He's getting pats on the back? Oh yeah, *'Nice one bro'*, like he's *so clever*, like he's a Proper Lad, like he's some Legend?!

> (**AARRON** *glitches again.*)

Urgh! I hate it! I bet he's loving it, getting all the attention, feeling so *proud* of himself!

AARRON. No, no it's not like that!

LEILAH. Yes it is Aarron, it always is!

> (**AARRON** *glitches and sees that* **BILLY** *sees it.*)

Boys are so stupid! So stupid!

> (**AARRON** *glitches, the biggest one yet, it goes on for ages. Sounds and lights supporting it. And when the glitch ends, we're in a suspended space.* **AARRON** *catches his breath, staring at* **BILLY***.*)

AARRON. What?

BILLY. Hurts doesn't it?

AARRON. What are you /

> *(He glitches again, sudden and furious. He's frustrated by it, trying to control his body.)*

Argh!

BILLY. It'll keep happening.

AARRON. What?

BILLY. *(To everyone.)* We've *got* to speak our truth.

AARRON. Err, yeah, alright mate!

> *(He glitches again, sudden and furious. He's really frustrated by it.* **LEILAH** *and* **MAISY** *stare at* **AARRON**. *He turns to* **BILLY**, *who's waiting patiently.)*

Well, well what if I dunno how? It's not like they teach us that, is it?! Not like there's some class on that. Nah, just stupid stuff, like algebra and whatever.

> *(***BILLY*** *hands* **AARRON** *a microphone.)*

What? Oh. Nah! Nah I /.. I'm alright thanks.

> *(***BILLY*** *waits, holding the mic.)*

Nah. Nah, I can't!

BILLY. Yeah you can.

> *(***AARRON*** *reluctantly takes the mic. He stares at us, embarrassed.* **BILLY** *starts making a track live.* **LEILAH** *and* **MAISY** *hear it.)*

MAISY. Erm? *What* are you doing?!

LEILAH. Is this a new bit?

MAISY. No, it's an interruption. Billy what the hell? We're not *rehearsing*! The audience is right there /

BILLY. Yeah exactly! Look, by repeating the stereotypes we're perpetuating them. What if we actually *did* something with this opportunity? What if we actually said something honest? Something true?!

AARRON. I can do that?

MAISY. No, you can't! There's a script for a reason! The writer will have carefully constructed the story, the character arc and, and everything! We can't just /

> (**BILLY** *turns up the music.* **AARRON** *glitches.*)

Stop! You can't do that, I said, stop! You can't do that!

> (**BILLY** *hits a button and replays* **MAISY**'s *last line.* **BILLY** *remixes it into the track.*)

LEILAH. Hey!

> (*'Hey' gets added too.* **BILLY** *hands* **AARRON** *the mic.* **AARRON** *turns to us, looking nervous.*)

AARRON. Okay. Okay. *(He glitches.)* Oh nah I dunno what I wanna say!

BILLY. You do! Just speak truth, to like, younger you.

AARRON. Okay, okay yeah. Okay younger me. Right, like, like yeah I dunno where we learnt this, I dunno who's to blame. But like, the whole system's messing with my brain. Younger me, just tryna be free but I'm stuck, can't you see? Not supposed to be, seen as weak, boys knee deep, in toxic masculinity, hide all vulnerability, disguise human fragility, cus boys don't cry, so wipe them eyes, be strong be a soldier, man up and shoulder, the burden of those emotions you bottle up, bottle up, bottle up 'til they burst up and over! Seriously man, it's a mess! I'd be laughing if this shit was funny.

BILLY. Knock knock.

AARRON. Who's there?

BILLY. The gender binary is a joke.

AARRON. Oh!

BILLY. I dunno who it was that wrote, the rules, don't wanna rock the boat but /

AARRON. We're out of tune on every note /

BILLY. Out of date, grab your coats!

AARRON. I don't remember getting a vote?!

BILLY. Listen, nearly seven billion people on the planet, and you only give us /

BILLY & AARRON. Two options?!

AARRON. Girl /

BILLY. Or boy?

AARRON. Pink /

BILLY. Or blue toys?

AARRON. Nah, don't be silly, like, seriously are you mad?

BILLY. Look, I'm not a lady, not quite a lad. Not a he, not a she, just me, just tryna be, the best me, I can be. So you can take your hyper-femininity, take your toxic masculinity, take your patriarchy-shaped humanity and leave me be /

AARRON. Jheeze!

BILLY. Look, I'm struggling to see how you can't see what I can see. You blind?

AARRON & BILLY. Open your eyes!

BILLY. The truth's crystal clear, old gender roles have gotta get outta here.

AARRON. The whole system needs a reboot, refresh, restart. Revolution's possible, hear me share from the heart. See us youngers? Online scrolling, always visible.

But the Truth is I feel invisible. The youth of today
have got *so much* to say but no one's listening. No one's
witnessing. No one's being truly honest! Sharing their
insides, too obsessed with glossy outsides. With shiny
screens, it's wild, tryna peak, like oops, I think my brain
cells leaked, out, don't freak, out, just rinse and repeat
out, the same shit over and over. Copying our fathers
and their fathers and theirs. An absent dad still shapes
who I am as a man. Yeah. That shit stings to say, but it's
true. *(To* **BILLY***.)* Hard to own that *I'm* scared. Far easier
to hate on *you*. With your, fluidity, and your freedom,
that's too much for my binary brain to understand.
(To everyone.) So I'm scrolling tryna find me a father
figure, tryna figure this shit out, copying what I see on
screens. Playing the role of 'man' but this performance
you see is only surface deep, hiding the true me. See
we're all stuck in a straitjacket of masculinity /

BILLY. The unwritten rules of our society /

AARRON. Touch screens lost touch with reality, disconnect
from my humanity, lost my authenticity /

BILLY. Dazzled by celebrities /

AARRON. R.I.P. integrity, we forgot that vulnerability
ain't weak. Jheeze! I'll repeat, said, we forgot that
Vulnerability Ain't Weak.

>   *(Music cuts.* **AARRON** *is buzzing.* **LEILAH** *and*
>   **MAISY** *are shocked.)*

MAISY. Woah! That was really great!

LEILAH. Yeah it was! Incredible!

AARRON. Ah, thanks babes /

LEILAH. Incredible, how you don't speak like that with
me?! Oh nah, I just get bare mumbles and grunts and /

AARRON. Grunts? /

LEILAH. Literally have to dig it out of you to get even the most basic bit of communication?!

AARRON. Yeah well /

LEILAH. And even then it's just surface-level shit?

AARRON. Nah cus /

LEILAH. Never like, actual honesty /

AARRON. Yeah cus you don't let me speak!

LEILAH. Excuse me?

AARRON. Can't barely get a word in!

LEILAH. I don't think /

AARRON. And you don't really listen! You don't actually really listen!

LEILAH. *(Fierce.)* Say somethin' worth listening to, Aarron, and maybe I will.

　　　　(Awkward silence.)

MAISY. Right. Well, maybe, we could start the speech with a quote? From, from erm, Shakespeare? Or. Or we could /

BILLY. Maisy?

MAISY. Or, or yeah, the history of love letters and how, how sexting is basically the modern equivalent /

BILLY. Maisy?

MAISY. Or we could begin with the definition of /

LEILAH. *MAISY!* Shut the hell up!

MAISY. I just /

LEILAH. Oh Maisy please! Go find *someone* to get off with! *Anyone!* Then you can actually join in this conversation about sex rather than saying such stupid shit!

MAISY. I'm not /

LEILAH. Seriously! If you go *get some*, you might be less uptight!

> (*Silence.* **LEILAH** *scrolls on her phone.* **MAISY** *tries to focus on her rewriting.* **LEILAH** *looks at the clock. Her body suddenly glitches, short and intense, unseen by anyone but* **BILLY**. **LEILAH** *turns away from* **BILLY**, *embarrassed they can see her glitch.* **LEILAH** *paces the room.* **MAISY** *looks up, annoyed.*)

MAISY. Do you have to? I'm trying to write this /

LEILAH. I'm trying to think! I need to get a message to Cherrelle. Or she's gonna think I've bailed on her.

MAISY. Can't you just text her?

LEILAH. Can't! She's /

LEILAH & AARRON. Not got her phone.

MAISY. Oh dear. *(Under her breath.)* How will she survive?

LEILAH. What?

MAISY. Nothing.

AARRON. Leilah.

> (**LEILAH** *is suddenly right in* **MAISY**'s *face.*)

LEILAH. Nah you've clearly got somethin' you wanna say. Some nasty little comment about my friend?

MAISY. No, no I really /

LEILAH. What is your problem?!

> (**MAISY**'s *body builds in a glitch.* **LEILAH** *stares at her.* **MAISY** *suddenly grabs the mic off* **BILLY** *and coughs and splutters up this truth to us.*)

MAISY. C-c-c-can't, c-c-c-can't you see? Girls have gotta be, either hypersexual or we're invisible? Clear consequences of terrible sex education, but the whole nation's too embarrassed to change the conversation? Refuse to even mention menstruation, or masturbation? The next generation will repeat the same shitty sensations of being shamed without hesitation, argh hear my frustrations at being female! Teaching me to hate my body? Hate my monthly bleeding? Hate my desires so much I ignore what I'm needing? Hate my shape or size or skin, the shame police swoop in, not even Christian but still feel soaked in sin. Too flirty or frigid for him, too fat or too thin, how's a girl meant to win?! *(To* **LEILAH**.*)* Taught to compete on every, little, thing?! What's my problem? I'm scared! *(To everyone.)* Scared I'm not enough, or I'm too much. Scared I'm wasting my young years, which will ruin my future. Scared of failure, I *have* to win! Scared of success and the pressure *that'll* bring. Scared of this whole sex thing. There. I said it. And yeah, I know that's embarrassing to admit but truth is I'm just not ready, I'm not, and it seems like everyone else is. *(To* **LEILAH**.*)* And I know you're struggling, in different ways. But some of the shame's the same. None of us taught how to say the things we need to say. I wish we were kinder.

> *(Music cuts.* **LEILAH** *is suddenly right in* **MAISY**'s *face.)*

LEILAH. What is your problem?

MAISY. *(Big, fake smile.)* I don't have one Leilah. I'm just trying to write this /

LEILAH. Oh can you just shut up about that?! In fact, do us all a favour and shut up in general, yeah? No one likes you.

MAISY. .

AARRON. Don't be a bitch.

LEILAH. Don't talk to me.

>(**LEILAH***'s body glitches. Everyone sees it. She's embarrassed.*)

AARRON. Look, I know you're upset /

LEILAH. I'm not, I'm actually fine!

AARRON. Right, well d'you wanna tell your face cus /

LEILAH. Oh shut up Aarron! I said I'm fine!

>(*Her body glitches, despite her best attempts to stop it.*)

Argh! Just leave it!

AARRON. Okay! (*Referring to* **BILLY**.) But, you know you should try it. It feels better.

MAISY. Yeah. It does.

LEILAH. Oh please!

MAISY. It's okay to be scared /

LEILAH. I am *not* scared!

MAISY. Okay!

AARRON. What's going on with you? Leilah? Why you so angry with me?

LEILAH. You know why!

AARRON. No I don't! Tell me!

LEILAH. Do you really wanna do this here?

AARRON. I don't care about them.

LEILAH. .

AARRON. What's going on?

LEILAH. (*Hissed.*) You know what!

AARRON. No I don't!

LEILAH. *(Hissed.)* You do!

AARRON. No, I really don't! You seem so mad with me, and I have no idea /

LEILAH. Because of the other night! Because of what you did!

AARRON. Ah, nah, that wasn't a big deal?

LEILAH. No?!

> *(**LEILAH** moves away from him.)*

AARRON. Leilah?

LEILAH. .

AARRON. Leilah?

LEILAH. .

> *(**AARRON** and **LEILAH**'s bodies suddenly glitch. **BILLY** and **MAISY** make a track to underscore them. **LEILAH** and **AARRON** come together centre stage and dance, tender and sweet. **LEILAH** kisses **AARRON** all over, everywhere except his mouth. Behind her back he pulls out his phone and clicks on some porn. She stops kissing.)*

AARRON. What?

> *(**LEILAH** pulls away.)*

Babes?

LEILAH. .

AARRON. Babes I, I just thought, we could /

LEILAH. You know I don't /

AARRON. Okay /

LEILAH. I don't like it. It feels /

AARRON. Okay. That's fine! That's fine. Loads of people do it, but that's fine.

LEILAH. It just feels like you're saying /

AARRON. That's not what /

LEILAH. I'm not enough /

AARRON. You *know* that's not what's going on. I just thought it'd be hot.

LEILAH. Why's she have to be blonde?

AARRON. Babes /

LEILAH. Massive fake boobs?

AARRON. Listen. It's not like the same as /.. It's not the same /

LEILAH. Not the same as what?

AARRON. I dunno, I can't, I can't explain.

LEILAH. You *always* click on /

AARRON. No I /

LEILAH. You prefer that /

AARRON. No! I just /

LEILAH. You're *with me* but you prefer *that*?

AARRON. No!

(*His body glitches.*)

Argh! I can't explain!

LEILAH. Forget it, okay?!

(**LEILAH***'s body glitches.*)

AARRON. Leilah /

LEILAH. Just forget it!

*(Her body glitches hard. In the middle of the glitch, **BILLY** holds out the microphone to her, and she eventually grabs it. She suddenly bursts into song. The below monologue can be adapted into song lyrics.)*

Look at me don't look at me, look at me don't look at me, look at me but don't really see. I love being the maestro of my own image on screens, but in real life I long to be seen as me. The human being beneath, this Black skin, this female shape that I'm in. I'm a young Black woman, that should be a win. So why's life so tiring? I'm trying to enjoy my own sexual energy, embrace the blessed gifts God's bestowed on me. Look at me don't look at me, look at me don't look at me, look at me but don't really see. This body I'm in is a miracle, and I know I should be grateful. And don't get me wrong, the performance of femininity is fun to play most days, but sometimes I lose my way. Sometimes I get distracted by what it looks like, more than what it feels like. Look at me don't look at me, look at me don't look at me, look at me but don't really see. Editing truth, filtering facts. Sharing this carefully curated version of me. Constantly ducking your male gaze, stuck in your don't-be-too-much-or-we'll-punish-you cage. I have to be hyper femme, because I have to earn feeling safe. I have to police your desires for me. Can't be seen as a threat, or I'm a criminal. What's criminal is how much time I waste worrying about all this. See I look strong but I'm struggling. Look at me don't look at me, look at me don't look at me, look at me but don't really see. I'm a young black woman, that should be a win. So why is life so tiring?

*(Music cuts. **LEILAH** catches her breath. **AARRON** watches her.)*

AARRON. Why didn't you just tell me?

LEILAH. I tried to!

>*(The couple look at each other, tired and sad.)*

You never wanna talk.

AARRON. You never wanna listen.

>*(Silence. They stare at each other. So much to say, none of it said. **LEILAH** turns away, upset and trying not to be. **MAISY** stares at the floor, wide-eyed. **AARRON** kicks the side of a table, frustrated. **BILLY** watches him.)*

AARRON. *(To **BILLY**.)* Wot?

BILLY. .

AARRON. *(Half-arsed.)* Freak.

>*(**AARRON** looks away. Then **BILLY** does. Silence.)*

MAISY. Right. Well. We could use the school motto, as a way of, erm /

BILLY. Oh I've had enough of this!

>*(**BILLY** grabs **MAISY**'s script and rips out the last few pages. **MAISY** is horrified. **LEILAH** and **AARRON** cheer.)*

MAISY. Oh my god! *What* have you *done*?! No no no! We were almost at the ending! You can't rip it up! The writer will have considered all the beats and, you can't interrupt the /

BILLY. Oh yes, let me guess. More conflict building, more tension rising, until we reach a climax? Haven't you ever noticed that the traditional storytelling structure exactly matches the shape of a male orgasm?

MAISY. *(Stunned.)* What?!

LEILAH. Eww!

BILLY. Exactly! So I have boldly, and if I may say so, quite *brilliantly*, opened us up to new possibilities! I am queering the gaze on this storytelling! Freeing us from this hetero-ghetto bullshit script!

LEILAH. Yes!

MAISY. Okay then, so what's the ending?

BILLY. What?

MAISY. What's this brilliant new ending gonna be?

BILLY. I, I don't know.

MAISY. Exactly!

> *(A seed of panic is planted in **BILLY***'s body, *but they quickly get an idea.)*

That's *exactly* why we need to stick to the script! So, what I suggest, is we /

BILLY. Aarron?

AARRON. Yeah?

BILLY. Do the football story?

AARRON. What, now?

MAISY. No /

BILLY. Yeah, go on! It's well good! It's like, obviously the best bit of the play.

AARRON. Yeah? Yeah, okay. Okay yeah, cool! *(To us.)* Liam passed me the ball, and I crossed it to Hassim, who burst up the wing lightning quick, the fastest you've ever seen!

> *(The other three actors step up to the microphones and the loop pedals to provide a sound-scape underneath **AARRON**.)*

Hassim crossed it to me, landed right at my feet, took a beat, boy *breathe*!

> *(Everyone inhales and exhales into the microphones.)*

Look up, scan the pitch and I see, Jack's at the edge of the box waiting for me, swish! Volleyed up and over, landed right at his feet, then /

ALL. *Bang!*

AARRON. He hits it perfectly and /

ALL. *GOAL!*

AARRON. We're all going bonkers! Jack gets me in a headlock /

MAISY. *(As Jack.)* Love you mate!

AARRON. And my mouth's proper beaming. Then we're in the locker room, all /

LEILAH. Banter! And /

BILLY. Lynx Africa!

LEILAH & BILLY. Lads-lads-lads!

MAISY. And stinky socks.

AARRON. When suddenly there's this moaning? Like, proper sexual moaning, and we're all blushing like *what's that*?! One of the lads is playing some porn clip on his phone and, I don't wanna look I dunno why, but I feel a bit sick? But they're all looking at it and /.. The guy's proper being rough with her, his hand around her throat and, surely that must be hurting? But she's making all this noise like she's loving it and. I dunno. Then *shit*! Mr Jones! Hide the phone!

> *(We hear the door bang open.)*

LEILAH. *(As Mr Jones.)* Well done today boys! Good effort! Now hurry up and get dressed, no messin' about. Quick as you like please!

> *(We hear Mr Jones exit. The lads crack up laughing.)*

AARRON. And then someone, I think it was Hassim, said somethin' about Jack. And he didn't hear it so he's like /

MAISY. *(As Jack.)* What's that?

AARRON. And the lads are laughing and Jack's ears go red, like bright red. And I feel myself getting defensive like, Jack's literally my brother. So I'm like /

ALL. Wot's your problem?

AARRON. And then Lewis bloody Taylor pipes up, course he does, he's always got his stupid big nose in everyone's business. He stands up and in front of everyone and goes /

BILLY. *(As Lewis.)* Well Jack don't need porn, his girl's well up for it. Ain't that right Jack?

AARRON. And everyone was looking at Lewis is now looking at Jack, who suddenly can't look at no one. Looks at his T-shirt he's about to pull on and is like /

MAISY. *(As Jack.)* Leave it!

AARRON. But Lewis Taylor can't leave it. Lewis Taylor don't understand the definition of leaving anything, ever. So he cracks up laughing, jumps up on the bench and starts humping Hassim all like /

BILLY. *(As Lewis.)* Oh Cherrelle! Ah yeah Cherrelle, yeah yeah yeah!

AARRON. And everyone pisses themselves. And Jack thumps Lewis Taylor in the belly, wham, and he doubles up over cus Jack hits like a man. And I thought that was that, but Lewis Taylor is just getting started /

BILLY. *(As Lewis.)* Wot's up Jack? Dunno wot you're doing? Can't get it up? Can't please your girl? Oh poor old Cherrelle!

AARRON. And everyone laughs, and I'm about to say *leave it Jack*, when he goes /

MAISY. *(As Jack.)* Let's just say I ain't gettin' bad feedback.

AARRON. And with that he pulls out his phone, and reads this message like /

MAISY. *(As Jack.)* "Babes you make me moan. Always dreamt I'd have a man like you. Them other boys? They ain't got a clue. My girls are telling me they have to fake, I'm like nah, can't relate, Jack you make my legs shake."

AARRON. And everyone *ooohs*! And Lewis Taylor is stunned! Jack's like /

MAISY. *(As Jack.)* Yeah hush your gums! Tryna take the piss? Your girl ain't sending you pics like this!

AARRON. And Jack holds up his phone. Like he's holding a trophy. His pride gets the best of him, and he lets all his bros see, the private messages, the photos, he even plays a voice clip. And the whole time somethin' in my stomach feels sick. Like my animal body, knows before I do, that this ain't gonna end well, Jack's actions aren't true. Aren't honest, aren't respectful, ain't coming from love. He's chasing dumb attention, putting that up above, Cherrelle. Him and Cherrelle, had a pact made in trust. Now he's sacrificing privacy to show off his lust? And me? ...I did nothing. I could have said somethin', done somethin', and yet. I dunno, it's the one thing I'll always regret.

(We hear the door bang open.)

LEILAH. *(As Mr Jones.)* Hurry up lads!

AARRON. Shit! Mr Jones! And Jack panics like /

MAISY. *(As Jack.)* Quick! Give me my phone!

AARRON. But there's no time! So Lewis Taylor pockets Jack's phone. And none of us can prove it, but somehow we all know. That those intimate sexy messages, private to Jack from Cherrelle, would get shared 'for a laugh', and end up seen by the whole world.

> *(Music cuts.* **AARRON** *turns to see* **LEILAH** *staring at him. A beat builds slowly underneath them, menacing and ugly.)*

LEILAH. What the hell Aarron?!

AARRON. What?

LEILAH. You just *stood* there? You did *nothin'*?! I can't believe you didn't even /

AARRON. And you're totally innocent aren't you?!

> *(***AARRON****'s body glitches.)*

LEILAH. What?

AARRON. She's your best mate, you must have known she was sending him stuff like that? I mean, you've sent stuff to me so /

LEILAH. Oh my god!

> *(***LEILAH****'s body glitches. The beat builds.)*

MAISY. *(To* **BILLY***.)* Did you know? About Aarron?

BILLY. I suspected, but I wasn't sure /

LEILAH. Oh my god, is that why you told him to do it?

AARRON. What, like, tryna set me up?

BILLY. No!

AARRON. 'Do the football bit Aarron, it's the best bit of the play'?!

LEILAH. Oh my gosh!

>   (**AARRON***'s body glitches. The beat builds.*)

BILLY. No! I really didn't know for sure! I just thought /

MAISY. I should have rewritten the ending!

BILLY. What?

MAISY. I'm supposed to be a prefect! But I'm so, *so disconnected*, from my peers and I, I /

>   (*Her body glitches.*)

MAISY. Oh God! It's my fault we're in this mess!

LEILAH. No it's mine! I didn't answer! Cherrelle phoned me and I, oh god, I didn't answer!

AARRON. I didn't do anything, to help Jack, I did nothing! I just froze!

LEILAH. I dropped her call, when she needed me most?!

AARRON. When he needed me most?!

>   (**LEILAH**, **AARRON** *and* **MAISY***'s bodies glitch. The beat builds. They all turn out to us, pulsing on the spot.*)

BILLY. The truth is I /..

MAISY. The truth /..

LEILAH. To be totally honest /..

AARRON. I'm honestly /..

MAISY. The truth /..

LEILAH. The truth /..

AARRON. The truth /..

>   (*They all glitch. The beat is at its peak. The glitch in their bodies builds and builds and*

*builds until suddenly it stops. They all try
to say the unsayable, but it's stuck in their
throats, caught in their mouths, impossible to
speak. They try, again and again and again.
Then* **BILLY** *suddenly explodes into a huge
glitch. The other three stand, staring at* **BILLY***,
stunned.)*

BILLY. The truth, the t-t-t-truth is I /.. The truth /..

*(***BILLY***'s body glitches turn into a very
naturalistic panic attack. Everyone's a beat
late at noticing.)*

LEILAH. Billy?! You alright?!

AARRON. Oh my god!

*(***MAISY*** *shoves* **AARRON** *out of the way.*
MAISY *holds* **BILLY***'s hand, makes eye contact,
speaks gently.)*

MAISY. Breathe! Billy, breathe.

(They breathe together. **BILLY** *calms. It takes
as long as it takes.)*

BILLY. Sorry.

MAISY. It's okay! You okay?

BILLY. Yeah. Yeah I'm fine. I'm fine it just, happens sometimes.

MAISY. Maybe you should tell /

BILLY. They already know. My mum. And school. I'm on
medication.

MAISY. Okay.

BILLY. It's nothing it's just /

BILLY & MAISY. Anxiety. Yeah.

(Shy smiles. Silence. **AARRON** *gingerly steps forward.)*

AARRON. They okay?

MAISY. Yeah.

AARRON. I had no idea you were /.. Finding stuff, you know.

LEILAH. Yeah, you seem so confident!

BILLY. Yeah well, I'm not. Not always, it's /.. I dunno, it's really hard sometimes. Like, I'm just tryna be who I am, tryna, I dunno, work it all out?! So why've they gotta make everything so shit?! All the time?! And I'm protesting and writing letters and petitions and it's like none of it helps?! They don't give a shit? It's so scary when the people in charge aren't protecting you. I'm not an "issue" in a "culture war". I'm a real person. I'm 16! And there's fuck all I can do about it?! ...And no one round here gets me, literally no one! Everyone just treats me like I'm some freak? And every day at school it's like, all these shitty little messages, just constantly telling me I'm not normal? And like, sometimes I start to wonder if they're right and I'm being mental and, it'd just be easier if I was like everyone else and/

LEILAH. No. You know that's not /

BILLY. I know! But it's like, it's tiring! You know? I'm tired!

MAISY. Me too.

LEILAH. Yeah.

AARRON. Yeah. Really tired.

BILLY. *(To everyone.)* This performance? It's exhausting!

LEILAH. Hah! Yeah!

BILLY. I'm exhausted! So yeah, I stay online, a lot. Like basically all the time. Cus all my friends are online, all of them. I've never actually even met most of them in real life! So yeah sometimes it's like I sound really confident, cus I'm saying all the right stuff, cus I've read it all or I've watched it or whatever, but the truth is. The truth is I've not actually done any of it. I've never even been kissed.

AARRON. That's cool.

BILLY. What?

AARRON. There's no rush is there? It's cool.

LEILAH. *(Smiling at **AARRON**.)* Yeah babes, it is.

*(To **BILLY**.)* Come here!

> *(**LEILAH** grabs **BILLY** in a big bear hug. **BILLY** is grateful for it. **AARRON** looks to **MAISY**.)*

AARRON. Well done Maisy. That was good.

LEILAH. Yeah, well done Mais.

> *(**MAISY** smiles.)*

AARRON. So, what happens now? We've still gotta end this somehow.

LEILAH. Yeah. What's gonna be our big finale?

AARRON. I'm not dancing!

LEILAH. No, you really shouldn't.

AARRON. Cheeky! What 'bout this speech then?

MAISY. Fuck the speech!

LEILAH. *Maisy!*

> *(They all laugh.)*

MAISY. Well honestly I /.. I guess we've all been honest, right?

AARRON. Yeah but, what are we going to say tomorrow, in assembly?

LEILAH. Oh God!

MAISY. Let's just say the truth.

LEILAH. What's that then?

MAISY. Well, the truth /.. The truth is, erm /

BILLY. The truth is, the painful truth is that this whole thing could have been prevented! If we'd *all* been better educated.

AARRON. Yeah.

> (**AARRON** *starts making a track to underscore them.*)

BILLY. If facts were stated. Not syllabuses written by opinionated politicians. Who are like, editing reality /

MAISY. Ignoring technology?

BILLY. Yes! Clinging to some old Christian ideology?!

LEILAH. Yeah!

MAISY. Covering a whole nation in guilt!

AARRON. Giving voice to the haters.

BILLY. Yeah, cus LGBTQ might sound like alphabet soup /

AARRON. Unless one of them letters describes you. Then what you gonna do?

LEILAH. How you gonna learn that your desires are sane /

BILLY. When you're surrounded by silence /

MAISY. And hungover hate from Section 28?

BILLY. Yes! And now with Section 35, how am I meant to feel safe? When every day the government find new ways to use trans bodies as pawns in their political games?

LEILAH. How are girls meant to 'own their own bodies', when they're shamed for masturbation?

MAISY. Yes!

LEILAH. Sex Ed focused solely on male ejaculation?

MAISY. Urgh!

LEILAH. Choosing to Edit Out /

LEILAH & MAISY. Clitoral stimulation?

AARRON. Shiny screens got us over-stimulated, yet still you ignore the X-Rated on our mobile phones?

LEILAH. Click, swipe, hardcore fornication /

AARRON. Pornography in the pockets of children. And in the classroom?

MAISY. Barely some bare bones biology of heterosexual sex. No lessons on consent /

AARRON. Or emotions /

LEILAH. Or pleasure.

BILLY. Stiff upper lip British embarrassment blushing and bumbling through the birds and the bees.

AARRON. Got us on our knees begging for clear clarification! Without excuses or /

LEILAH. Justifications?

AARRON. Yeah! Just give it to us straight!

MAISY. Or queer?

BILLY. Yeah!

AARRON. Just, give it to us *honestly*?!

LEILAH. Yeah, tell us the truth!

BILLY. And don't be embarrassed. Please! Or all you're teaching me is to be ashamed.

AARRON. Yeah!

BILLY. And that's not me playing a blame game, but *your* shame is getting passed on to us and that's a fact.

LEILAH. Yeah but it was probably passed on to them.

MAISY. I mean I wouldn't wanna be a teacher.

AARRON. Nah!

LEILAH. Doing sex ed? Nah that's grim!

AARRON. Standing up in front of us /

MAISY. Trying not to blush /

AARRON. Tryna rush through these awkward conversations about sex /

LEILAH. Cus us rowdy young ones ain't making your job any easier let's be honest.

BILLY. No way!

AARRON. Nah but, who left the teachers hanging out to dry like that?

MAISY. Yeah, why aren't they supporting you more?

LEILAH. Yeah, cus it's like, like over-worked and under-paid teachers, tryna jump through hoops, back-dated and gated, feel jaded. Governments painted over facts/

MAISY. Turned a blind eye to the essentials, like /

MAISY & LEILAH. 'Boys will be boys' /

LEILAH. And that's that?

AARRON. Yeah, you really gonna point the finger at Cherrelle and Jack?!

MAISY. Young couple sexting, *'let themselves down'*?

AARRON. Nah, come on now! Take some responsibility, please!

MAISY. Yeah, we're not some statistics in a government survey. We're real people /

BILLY. Let down by a system that's failing.

LEILAH. Yeah!

BILLY. The system is failing, all of us. Queer or straight. Young or old. Teacher or student. Everyone. And it's really vital that we change it, and it's really urgent. Cus like, sorry to sound so epic about it but, yeah, it is epic. Like, I genuinely think it'd be healing for the whole world. Cus what we're really talking about is learning how to have honest communication, like how to speak about difficult scary vulnerable things. How to talk honestly about sex. Which is really about pleasure, and power and safety and joy and consent and that'd be so healing for everyone! Like, the negative ripple effect is clearly so huge! So if we could change it tomorrow, then like, the positive effect could be huge! How you feel about yourself, and your sexuality, and your identity and your body and how you are as a human having healthy relationships with other humans. And how to see each other, as we really are, and respect each other. I mean, wow, what a beautiful thing that'd be like, why wouldn't we want to change that?!

LEILAH. Yeah it's time!

MAISY. It's time.

AARRON. It's time.

BILLY. OK, so, what now?

End of Play

ABOUT THE AUTHOR

Charlie Josephine is an actor and a writer. Their award-winning work includes *I, Joan*, *Bitch Boxer* and *Massive*. Charlie's passionate about honest, sweaty storytelling that centres working-class women and queer people. They're an associate artist at the NSDF and is this year's Resident Writer at Headlong Theatre. Charlie's currently under commission at the RSC, Salon Pictures, NT Connections and Pentabus Theatre.

Ingram Content Group UK Ltd.
Milton Keynes UK
UKHW020921070623
423006UK00010B/105